Panic Attack Survival Guide

Five simple, effective Treatments to help you *Never* panic again

by
Christine Maynard
and
Julia Higginbotham

ISBN 978-0-6152-1677-5

© 2008 Siton Youryoni Books

Published by Siton Youryoni Books

Please address all inquiries to
LittlestarTGSal@aol.com

PANIC ATTACK SURVIVAL GUIDE

"In boldness,

There is beauty, magic and Power

Take one step

And the Universe rushes to meet you"

Goethe

We have divided The Panic Attack
Survival Guide into five chapters.
Each chapter focuses on one logical,
powerful tool which we invite you to
integrate into your practice of daily
Living, to effect the change you seek.

This offering was created because we
believe that you *can* find peace and
connection through these five,
straightforward measures. They have
worked, personally, for us, as well as
for students, peers, children and
friends.

Embrace this opportunity and feel a
shift toward serenity.

Love
Julia and Christine
May 2008

#1

"Be still and know that I am God"

These powerful, centering words

are found in Psalms 46:10. Most of us

constantly create, with our busy

monkey minds, escapism. We are

always onto....the next thing. If we

are physically in one place, but

mentally in another, then where are

we, really? We have placed ourselves

in limbo, a very uncomfortable place

to be. Anxiety is, in part, fearing our own center, our power seat. The awareness that there is more than just going through the motions of living scares us.

Sit or lie quietly and follow your breath, deeply and smoothly in, and gently releasing out. Speak, as you breathe at a pace with which you are comfortable, "Be still, and know that I Am God."

By the third time you repeat this powerful mantra you will feel God, the power of the entire beneficent Universe, commanding your body and mind to settle down. Saying these words creates a shift, felt soothingly, on a cellular level. Your entire body and mind will begin to soften into the security of being breathed, by God. A pervasive peace and stilling of all anxieties is the almost immediate result. Trust resonates. You will find

the capacity to laugh and to be happy

again, no longer lost in the illusion of

separateness, or the belief that we

alone manifest our destiny.

Breathing exercises strengthen

our inner energies and currents, our

God Self. The invisible flow, through

chakras and nadis, leads us to our

most powerful center, and we touch

something infinitely greater than who

or what we thought we were. From

that contact comes clarity and hope.

Touching the numinous and recognizing

it as our Self takes away all doubt,

leaving us with true empowerment.

Instead of contracting inward, we are

free to be bold, unleashing our true,

unique selves. Confident. Happy.

Connected to Source. Co-creators of

all.

#2

Relax your face and pelvic floor

This is the first step in any yoga posture, and, as a yogini (Dynamic Yoga Training Method,) this simple release has changed my life. I remind myself to relax throughout the day, for relaxation takes practice.

Repetition. Closing off these opposite poles of the body by holding tension in the face and retention in the pelvic floor creates an

environment in which stress

flourishes.   By relaxing these two

poles of the body, face and pelvic

floor, everything in between releases.

The body, therefore the mind, is

immediately able to experience a

deeper level of relaxation.

One's connection to life is felt

much more readily when the face and

pelvic floor are relaxed. Breathing

becomes free and easy as air is

allowed to move deeper into the lungs,

filling the abdomen. The attendant

feeling of groundedness and

centeredness will dissolve a panic

attack, as energy that was held and

blocked flows freely. This openness

allows the magic, beauty, and power of

the Universe to enter us,

transforming our lives.

Babies naturally relax their pelvic floors and faces because they do not know that they should do differently. Retention is a societal construct, partially arising from toilet training. When you relax your pelvic floor, it doesn't mean your bowels empty, they just relax. By also relaxing the face, the entire core of the body becomes soft, and the mind is no longer harsh, compartmentalized.

I invite you to try this practice

right now, wherever you are. It

doesn't matter if you're sitting,

standing, or lying down. This release

can be done at any time. Simply relax,

release, pacify the muscles of your

face and pelvic floor (anus). Take as

long as you need, without self-

judgment, to do this. It is a subtle,

small shift, allowing alignment. It may

take several breaths and a little

concentration if you've never tried it before. Once you feel relaxed in your face and pelvic floor, take an easy, extended inhalation and allow it to move deeply into your lungs and abdomen. Then, allow your exhalation to easily complete itself, without forcing the air out. With relaxed face and pelvic floor, continue to take easy, free breaths, and you will feel tension and panic immediately leave

your body and mind.

Now you are primed to move

through fear. If you ever feel lost in

panic, you can find your place in the

Universe again by bringing relaxation

to the face and pelvic floor, and

simply breathing.

#3

Be grateful and you will taste the sweetness

"Thank you, God, for the gift of awareness." Those of us who suffer with depression and anxiety which lead to panic, are actually suffering from heightened awareness. We often panic because we know not where to go with the energy. We try to put it to sleep, to numb. Yet its beauty is staggering, if we are brave enough to look upon it in its entirety, not pulling away from what we have labeled "bad." Not crossing our fingers in hopes of drawing that which we consider "good." Simply being. Simply being grateful.

The highest awareness is always present if we put our full attention toward it, with gratitude, for all we experience. As my father taught me,

"Love mightily; practice loving every living being. Really practice."

When we open fully, we have the strength to know joy and pain, ecstasy and sorrow, and to be equally grateful for all states, all experiences and lessons.

Write a thank you God note when you feel centered, and express potent gratitude for what is in your life right now. Then, still writing in the present tense, thank God for what you would like to have, as if the things you desire are already active and present in your life. Aim carefully.

Read what you have written to yourself a few times a day, for at least three days. Then, fold it up, and put it away. The Universe is working for you, as a co-creator with God. You are magnetically drawing to you that which you envision. Gratitude is

simply the fuel.

Gratitude changes our vibration

through a not so subtle shift; we

become aware of something deeper at

work within us, and we partner with

that Energy. Gratitude is the

opposite of contraction of energy. It

allows us to move beyond ego into a

state of freedom. Freedom from all

of our disturbances. All of our fears.

It allows us to accept our lives as they are, and to respond with genuine appreciation and love.

* When you script your future, be grateful, in advance. Picture the thing you desire happening, your reaction to it and others' reactions to your reaction of having your dreams come true.

"If you want to shrink something, you must first allow it to expand. If you want to get rid of something, you must first allow it to flourish."

                    Tao Te Ching

#4

Practice moving through panic

This exercise is the fast track to healing; it is the most viscerally felt, and, the most mentally demanding of the five approaches proffered. If you are brave enough for this "Navy Seal" training to release suffering, let's go. Roll up your sleeves, and don't slip the punches.

If you want to get rid of the panic and the panic over nearly panicking, then face it. Turn on your heels and tell it to unzip itself and face you in its smallness, in its irrelevance, in its no-thing-ness. When you've had enough to be very clear that you don't choose or need any more suffering in order to find redemption, atonement, peace, you can stop panic.

Jesus' suffering as redemption didn't provide us with a "get out of suffering free card," as modern Christianity sometimes spins it. He showed us the Way, how to achieve epiphanies, enlightenment, and an end to suffering, through *willingness* to take the cup. He showed us how to end suffering by feeling it fully.

"I don't want this, God, but if it is Your Will, as it must be, or it wouldn't be happening, then bring it on!"

Suffering gets a bad rap. Ending suffering is only achievable IF one has been vulnerable and willing to become one with the suffering, the very suffering most of us take great measures to insure that we will avoid.

There are never guarantees of safely laid floorboards on which to rest one's feet. Don't seek suffering

out, but when it comes, open widely

the gates and pull suffering in like a

long lost lover, kissing it on the lips.

To break down this koan of

escaping the fear of suffering panic

attacks through creating enough

vulnerability to feel the suffering,

simply let yourself do whatever begins

them and adamantly SIT and do not

pick up the phone or take diazepam or

act scared or go through, mentally, a

thousand escape routes which is

pointless and futile, anyway.

The following visualizations can

be utilized to induce a "homeopathic"

dose of panic:

Feel the feeling of the Universe

expanding so rapidly you lose your

place and cannot retrieve it. Feel the

coldness of your insides and the

fullest manifestation of aloneness.

Perhaps it is experienced as being

catapulted at the speed of light above

every puka (hole) in every coral on

every reef, and you just might fall

into any one of those holes, forever,

which could be insanity or lostness, or

your specific brand of suffering.

There. Did that do it? Did you

feel the beginning of the fear? Fight

or flight?

Good, keep sitting. Keep

breathing. Bring your full awareness

to your fear and stay there, for as

long as it takes, and you will see, (if

you are willing to stay present,) that

there is an end to suffering. You run

smack into a wall and the panic simply

dissolves and you are left with its

opposite. Oneness. Love.

Connectedness. Beauty. Peace. The

Holy Comforter. It really works.

There is an end to panic, and inherent in the panic is its opposite. Discover it.

The fear is vacuous. Powerless. You are an entity in a body, who has love, guidance, blessings, gifts and promises you made before you incarnated, to bravely fulfill. So open to your brand of fear fully, and take back your power. Remember- the mind is a terrible master and a wonderful servant. Ride fear like a

bronco, stay with it, and be amazed to

witness it dissolve.

"There is no fear in love,
but perfect love casteth out
fear."

John 1:18

#5

Becoming comfortable with death

stops panic attacks

I have discovered that one can also work on finding safety, ease of being and acceptance within the irrefutable fact that life ends! It was the most wonderful experience I've had, the dying. Find out what scares you about it. The loss of others? Worries about children?

Being alone? Or suffering, the

anguish of what might precede

release?

Think about the end of your life

as being blissful, rewarding and

peaceful. Live in a fashion which

insures that you have no regrets, that

you have not been thoughtless, or

hurtful. Or insincere.

Commit to treating yourself with

the utmost dignity, to being brave

enough to live life openly. Envision

with confidence having fulfilled your

soul's promises while in your body, in

this life.

Picture a gentle release and all

those you love who have gone before,

angels and spirit guides, too, greeting

you. Imagine an end to the tedium of

time, and man made thought

constructs. Envision the clear end to

all neuroses, knowing that your Light

will shine with no covering, no concern

for appearances, and will be

recognized, seen and met by all Light.

Practice breathing and feel the

breath, especially the end point of a

full inhalation, before you exhale, as

well as bringing awareness to the end

point of each full exhalation.

Observe. Feel the invisible pulse of

all life force, breathing until you feel

you are being breathed by God. For

you ARE. And you will feel perfect

love, which is the opposite of FEAR.

You may access esoteric

knowledge and deep intuition; you may

have mystical experiences and

epiphanies through these practices.

Embrace and learn from whatever

occurs. Be grateful, and open. And,

when there are troubles and conflicts,

don't buy into them, allowing fear to

prance through your door and set up

shop.

Feel brave, strong and open, for

you ARE. And, always remember; the

closer you are to the Light, the less

the blind can see you.

Written with Love

Inspired by Spirit

You can reach the authors, Christine

Maynard and Julia Higginbotham at

LittlestarTGSal@aol.com

"I wish that Life

Should not be cheap, but sacred.

The days to be as centuries,

Loaded, fragrant."

Rilke

ISBN 978-0-6152-1677-5

www.ingramcontent.com/pod-product-compliance
Lightning Source LLC
Chambersburg PA
CBHW030306030426
42337CB00012B/603